OXFORD PLAYSCRIPTS

Wakefield Libraries & Information Services

Carol

kens

Kidd
olds

OXFORD
UNIVERSITY PRESS

Great Clarendon Street, Oxford OX2 6DP

Oxford University Press is a department of the University of Oxford. It furthers
the University's objective of excellence in research, scholarship, and education by
publishing worldwide in

Oxford   New York

Auckland   Cape Town   Dar es Salaam   Hong Kong   Karachi
Kuala Lumpur   Madrid   Melbourne   Mexico City   Nairobi
New Delhi   Shanghai Taipe   Toronto

With offices in

Argentina   Austria   Brazil   Chile   Czech Republic   France   Greece
Guatemala   Hungary   Italy   Japan   Poland   Portugal   Singapore
South Korea   Switzerland   Thailand   Turkey   Ukraine   Vietnam

Oxford is a registered trade mark of Oxford University Press
in the UK and in certain other countries

British Library Cataloguing in Publication Data

Data available

ISBN 978 019 839040 4

10 9 8 7 6 5 4 3 2 1

Typeset in India by TNQ Books and Journals Pvt. Ltd.

Printed in Great Britain by Bell and Bain Ltd, Glasgow.

Acknowledgements

Script originally commissioned by Creation Theatre Company, Oxford
The Publisher would like to thank Jenny Roberts for writing the Activity section.

Cover images © V. J. Matthew / Shutterstock; Dm_cherry / Shutterstock

Image of Charles Dickens © Pictorial Press Ltd / Alamy

Artwork by Neil Chapman

CONTENTS

WHAT THE ADAPTERS SAY

In December 2009 Richard approached me and suggested that we write an adaptation of *A Christmas Carol* for a local theatre company. After a hastily-written first draft, the producer of the company organized a reading of the script with a group of actors. Following the read-through, the company arranged for a research and development week (a week where, like the name suggests, we scrutinized and developed the ideas in the script). This took place in the middle of spring – the sun was shining, birds were chirping, and two writers, four actors and a director were locked in a basement room of a church trying to feel Christmassy!

This was, however, an invaluable aid to the development of the script. We explored the characters' pasts, looked at *how* they had got to where they were in the story and most importantly, *why*. We re-read key parts of the novella, exploring exciting and original ways to retell this most familiar of stories to a modern audience. At the end of five days, we were left exhilarated and absolutely clueless as to where to start the rewriting! During the rewriting process, we were in constant contact with the producer and the director of the show, discussing and refining ideas. We tore large chunks of the script apart, re-examined characters and ideas, and ended up with something very, very different from what we had written before. Over the following months, more suggestions were made, new people were consulted, more rewrites were completed and *finally,* ten months after we had started writing (and *ten drafts later*), we dotted the final 'i' and crossed the final 't', and our script was complete.

The most important thing you must know about this script (or any script) is that it is best appreciated in performance. We wrote this script so that it would be performed, and the process of writing it for performance involved so many people – writers, producers, directors, designers, actors, stage managers, and many more. The fact that we were commissioned by a theatre company meant that we had to consider what it was that they wanted us to write and try to write something that all parties were comfortable with. It was sometimes difficult to compromise – they would feel strongly about things and so would we, but the nature of putting together a performance is about finding a solution that works for everyone. What feels best for a writer may not always be best for the audience watching it. What feels best for an actor playing a part may not always be best for the director. It is a complex dynamic and the role we played as writers was a challenging one.

Something that worked both for us and against us was the popularity of the story. It is a story that *everyone* knows. From the Dickens novella itself to the dozens of film adaptations (including the much-loved Muppets version), everyone has grown up with a version of this story which they consider to be definitive. Any audience going to see *A Christmas Carol* has certain expectations – Marley weighed down by chains, the Ghost of Christmas Future bedecked with an enormous black cloak, and a larger than life Ghost of Christmas Present. They know what they want from the story, and as writers we faced the problem of meeting these expectations while also doing something original.

The one very noticeable change we made to the story was the ending. In Dickens's version, Scrooge is reformed and vows to Cratchit that he will be a better man and a better boss. Then, he sends him off to buy a coal scuttle so that he may add fuel to the fire … and that's it! After all the years of torment, Cratchit's big reward at the end is a new coal scuttle! Richard suggested that this simply wasn't enough and proposed that the only way Scrooge could make it up to him was if he made Cratchit a partner in the business – a fitting reward for all Cratchit's sufferings.

At the end of such an extensive writing process, we can be sure that our script has been thoroughly considered. We have scrutinized each character and painstakingly chewed over every last detail of plot to ensure that our script is faithful to the novella and pays homage to that unmistakeable Dickensian style. We hope that we have given readers (and actors, directors and audiences of future performances) food for thought.

Conor McReynolds and Richard Kidd

About the Author

Regarded by many as the greatest Victorian novelist, Charles John Huffam Dickens was born in Portsmouth on 7 February 1812, the son of a clerk of the Navy Pay office. Having had the good fortune to be sent to school at the age of 9, he was forced to leave school when he was 12 to work in a factory after his father was imprisoned for debt. These childhood experiences of factory work and poverty were significant influences on his later writing.

Charles Dickens was a prolific writer. As well as authoring 15 novels and many short stories and articles, Dickens edited a weekly journal for 20 years. During his life he was remarkably popular, indeed famous, in part through his lectures and social campaigning. But it was mainly through his novels that immediate and lasting fame came to Dickens. Publishing his novels often in small instalments, he created some of the most striking and memorable characters, storylines and settings in literary history.

A Christmas Carol is arguably Dickens's most well-known, and certainly amongst children, best loved short story (or novella); it has consistently attracted adaptations ever since it was first published in 1843.

Charles Dickens had 10 children and died on 9 June 1870. He is buried in Poet's Corner in Westminster Abbey in London, reflecting the impact he had on the nation both as a writer and a campaigner for children's rights.

A Note on Staging

If you are considering staging this script, it is important to
remember that it moves from place to place and from time to
time very quickly. This makes it impossible to have elaborate,
detailed sets for each location. There is one location, however,
which the whole story revolves around – Scrooge's apartment.
This is where he first encounters Marley, it is where he meets
the Ghosts of Christmas Past and Present, and where, at the
end of a long night, he makes the decision to turn his life
around. It is a place of great importance, and for this reason we
suggest reserving one section of the stage for use as Scrooge's
apartment throughout.

The rest of your set can be very simple – if you set out
two desks with a candle on each and a 'Scrooge & Marley' sign
above them the audience will know where you are. If you push
those two desks together, put a tablecloth over them, place a
small turkey on top and lean a crutch against one of the chairs
the audience will know where they are. Keep it simple and be
confident that the audience will be able to follow what you are
doing if you do it with enough conviction!

There are so many parts in this script – you could perform
it with as few as seven people and as many as 31. Obviously,
the one constant of the story is Scrooge (he features in all but
one scene in the script). It would be a huge ask for one person
to play Scrooge the whole way through and so you might
consider role-sharing for this part. The easiest way to do this is
with a piece of token costume; it might sound strange, but the
audience will follow what you are doing! It could be as simple
as the actor playing Scrooge wearing a nightcap or a coat, or
carrying a prop like a money bag. When an actor is playing
that part, they wear or carry the token costume. This becomes
a symbol that the audience associate with the character, and
it means that one actor does not have to carry the weight of
responsibility that comes with playing a role as large as Scrooge
for the entire performance.

COSTUME AND PROPS

How a director or designer interprets this script is entirely up to them. You can use as little or as much as you want in terms of set, props and costume – use your imagination and make the script come to life however you see fit. While we would never encourage you to rely on props or costume to tell your story (no amount of props, costumes or effects can replace good storytelling from committed actors), below are a few items that will add a little something extra to your performance.

Act 1, Scene 1: **The offices of Scrooge & Marley**

COSTUME: Hat, coat and scarf for Cratchit
Scarf for Fred
Hat for Carol-singing Boy
Coat and hat for Scrooge

PROPS: Door to office
'Scrooge & Marley' sign
Two desks
Two chairs
Paperwork
Candles
Coins
Clock
Fireplace
Sack of coins containing series of ever-smaller money bags

Act 1, Scene 2: **The streets of London; Scrooge's apartment**

COSTUME: Top hat, coat and scarf for Scrooge
Nightgown and nightcap for Scrooge later in the scene
Chains for Marley

PROPS: Keys
Scrooge's apartment door and window
Two chairs in front of the fireplace
Bowl of gruel
Lights (that can flicker)
Bed with curtains
Poker
Clock
Mirror

Act 1, Scene 3: **Scrooge's apartment; a country lane; an old schoolhouse; Mr Fezziwig's office; another office**
COSTUME: Nightgown and nightcap for Scrooge
Costume for Ghost of Christmas Past
Hat and jacket for Mr Fezziwig
Dress for Belle
Dress for Mrs Fezziwig
School dress for Fan
PROPS: Bedroom props as in Act 1, Scene 2
Desk
Paperwork
Coins

Act 1, Scene 4: **Scrooge's apartment; Cratchit's home; Fred's home; a deserted place**
COSTUME: Nightgown and nightcap for Scrooge
Costume for Ghost of Christmas Present
Shorts and jacket for Tiny Tim
Dress and apron for Mrs Cratchit
Hat, jacket and shirt for Bob Cratchit
Dress for Martha
Festive hats and dresses for Fred and party guests
PROPS: Bedroom props as in Act 1, Scene 2
A large bottle
Chairs
Table (two desks pushed together)
Tablecloth

Gravy boat
Bowls of vegetables
Plates
Cutlery
Glasses
A *very* small turkey
A loaf of bread
Tim's crutch and wooden horse
A carving knife
Glasses for party guests
Small pieces of paper for game

Act 2, Scene 1: **The streets of London; a pawn shop; Cratchit's home; a graveyard**

COSTUME: Nightgown and nightcap for Scrooge
Black hooded cloak for the Ghost of Christmas Future
Replica of Scrooge's outfit

PROPS: Washing line, rags and a smouldering fire
A bag of money
Mrs Cratchit's knitting
Furniture props for Cratchit's home as in Act 1, Scene 4
A gravestone

Act 2, Scene 2: **Scrooge's apartment**
COSTUME: Nightgown, nightcap, slippers, shirt and tie for Scrooge
Shirt, jacket, shorts and hat for boy

PROPS: Bedroom props as in Act 1, Scene 2
Coin

Act 2, Scene 3: **Cratchit's home**
PROPS: Furniture props for Cratchit's home as in Act 1, Scene 4
Small presents wrapped in brown paper
A wooden horse and book
Tim's crutch
A giant turkey
A note

Act 2, Scene 4:	Fred's home
COSTUME:	Top hat, scarf, coat and walking stick for Scrooge
	Festive jackets, hats and dresses for party guests
PROPS:	Party props as in Act 1, Scene 4
	A blindfold

Act 2, Scene 5:	The offices of Scrooge & Marley
COSTUME:	Coat, hat and scarf for Scrooge
	Coat and hat for Cratchit
PROPS:	Office props as in Act 1, Scene 1
	The new sign wrapped up in paper ('Scrooge & Cratchit Associates: Working in loving memory of Jacob Marley')
	A dusty bottle

CHARACTER LIST

Ebenezer Scrooge   Owner of Scrooge & Marley; a selfish miser

Bob Cratchit   Scrooge's clerk

Ghost of Jacob Marley   Scrooge's former business partner

Ghost of Christmas Past

Ghost of Christmas Present

Ghost of Christmas Future

Fred   Scrooge's nephew

Elizabeth   Fred's wife

Young Ebenezer Scrooge   Scrooge as a young man

Fan Scrooge   Scrooge's sister and Fred's mother

Mr Fezziwig   Scrooge's former employer and mentor

Mrs Fezziwig   Mr Fezziwig's wife

Belle Winklesworth   Scrooge's former fiancée

Emily Cratchit   Bob Cratchit's wife

'Tiny Tim' Cratchit   Bob Cratchit's critically ill son

Martha Cratchit   Bob Cratchit's daughter

Old Joe   A pawnbroker

Mary   A thief

Charity Worker 1

Charity Worker 2

Party Guest 1

Party Guest 2

Party Guest 3

Merchant 1   Businessman acquainted with Scrooge

Merchant 2   Businessman acquainted with Scrooge

Merchant 3   Businessman acquainted with Scrooge

Ignorance & Want

Joseph Wiggins

Mr and Mrs Winterbottom

Carol-singing Boy

Delivery Boy

Carol Singers

Party Guests

ACT 1

SCENE 1

The offices of Scrooge & Marley.

Carol Singers enter singing Good King Wenceslas. *Bob Cratchit is leading them. They stop in front of the door of Scrooge & Marley. The Carol Singers sing under Cratchit's narration.*

Cratchit

[Narrating] Marley was dead, to begin with. There was no doubt whatever about that. He was, to use the parlance of our times, dead as a doornail. Personally, I would have been tempted to say 'dead as a coffin nail', for what piece of ironmongery can claim to have such a strong link to death as a coffin nail? No matter, it is not up to me, and we must say that Marley was 'dead as a doornail'. It is essential to our story that you understand that Marley was dead. If it were not for the fact that Marley was dead, there would be nothing so remarkable in the events of our tale. But he was dead, and luckily through establishing this fact, we should be able to find the wonder in this story.

Scrooge bursts through the door of Scrooge & Marley, turning his attention to the Carol Singers.

Scrooge	Humbug!

*The **Carol Singers** scatter, and **Scrooge** returns to his work station. **Cratchit** gathers up coins in a hat and goes towards his desk.*

Cratchit	*[Narrating]* Ebenezer Scrooge was an interesting sort of man. He wasn't necessarily the warmest of people; he rather preferred the cold. And for a person of considerable wealth, he wasn't inclined to share it with those in need. In fact, he had something of a reputation in London, both as a shrewd businessman … and as a miserly old git!
Scrooge	Bah! Quit your blathering, Cratchit! Now, get to work lest you spend your Christmas seeking alternative employment!
Cratchit	Yes, Mr Scrooge. Right away, Mr Scrooge.

*Cratchit runs in holding his hat with the money from the carol singing. **Scrooge** grabs the hat, tips the money out, and gives the hat back to **Cratchit**. **Cratchit** goes to his desk and immediately knuckles down to work. **Scrooge** spies on **Cratchit** as he works.*

[Narrating] Unlike most people, Scrooge hated it when the office was cosy and warm, for the piercing cold was a reminder of all the money he was saving on coal for the fires! The only thing Scrooge hated more than Christmas was people, so it was rather unfortunate then, for old Ebenezer, when his nephew entered the office with a friendly—

Fred enters.

Fred	Merry Christmas, Uncle! Merry Christmas, Bob Cratchit!
Cratchit	Merry Christmas to you, Fred! How is your lovely wife?
Fred	Radiant as ever, my dear man. And give my very best to your darling family.
Cratchit	Many thanks, Fred. And I—
Scrooge	One more word out of you, Cratchit, and I shall make good on yesterday's threat to use your wage packet as fuel for the fire.

*Cratchit falls silent and puts his head down to work once again. **Fred** approaches **Scrooge's** desk.*

Fred	Come now, Uncle! Where's your festive spirit? Have you forgotten what day it is?
Scrooge	It is a Friday, and in this office it is a regular working day, unlike the rest of this godforsaken city.
Fred	Come now, Uncle Ebenezer, you know full well it is Christmas Eve! And I'm quite sure you know why I am here. Every year I come here on December 24th, hoping that you will join me and my darling wife for a spot of Christmas dinner, and every year you say—
Scrooge	You keep Christmas in your way, Frederick, and I will keep it in mine.
Fred	But you don't keep it, Uncle! I'm quite sure you'll sit in your armchair before your half-hearted fire, eating your usual bowl of gruel. Join us, Uncle, please! We have ordered a sumptuous goose, and as many bottles of fine wine and cider as you could imagine getting through in one day!
Scrooge	What would compel a man to spend a full month's wages on a nonsense such as Christmas?
Fred	It's Christmas! What more does one need to be merry?
Scrooge	Merry? What reason have you to be merry? You're poor enough.
Fred	What reason have you to be miserable? You're rich enough!
Scrooge	You have said your piece, sir, and I shall now say mine. It sickens me to see fools such as you, up to your necks in debt, prancing around this Earth pretending that just for a day there are no problems, that everything is merry and light. If I could work my will, every idiot who goes about with 'Merry Christmas' on his lips should be boiled with his own pudding, and buried with a stake of holly through his heart. Good afternoon.
Fred	There is good to be had in the company of others, you would do well to remember that.

Scrooge	What good can be had in the company of others? Does company put food on your table? No, it does not. Much good has it ever done you!
Fred	There are many things in life which do not yield a profit. And although Christmas has never put a scrap of gold or silver in my pocket, I believe it has done me good and I say God bless it!
	Cratchit, overcome by the power of **Fred***'s speech, stands and applauds. Under* **Scrooge***'s venomous look he attempts to make it look like he was swatting a fly or warming his hands or some other feeble cover-up.*
Scrooge	You're quite a powerful speaker, sir. It's a wonder you don't go into Parliament.
Fred	You'll come then?
	Scrooge ignores **Fred***, and continues with his work.*
	Uncle Ebenezer, I want nothing of you. I ask nothing of you. Tell me, please, why can we not be friends?
	Fred offers his hand, but **Scrooge** *ignores him entirely.* **Fred** *re-gathers his energies to make one final attempt.*
	We have never had a quarrel to which I have been a party. However, I have made a trail in homage to Christmas, and I will keep my Christmas humour to the last. Merry Christmas, Uncle.
Scrooge	Bah! Humbug.
Fred	And a Happy New Year!
	Charity Worker 1 and **Charity Worker 2** *enter the office, interrupting* **Fred***.* **Fred** *puts on his scarf and goes towards the exit.*
Charity Worker 1	Good day, sir. Do I have the pleasure of addressing Mr Scrooge or Mr Marley?
Fred	Neither, sir. I am just leaving, but you will find Mr Scrooge behind his desk. A Merry Christmas to you! The offer stands, Uncle. Merry Christmas, Mr Cratchit!

Cratchit	Merry Christmas, Fred!

Scrooge turns to Fred, impatiently.

Scrooge	Good afternoon!

Fred exits. Charity Worker 1 approaches Scrooge's desk.

Charity Worker 1	Mr Scrooge, I assume? A pleasure to make your acquaintance.
Charity Worker 2	And … Mr Marley?

The Charity Workers look at Cratchit, who shakes his head.

Charity Worker 1	I see … Mr Marley has left for Christmas already?
Scrooge	No.
Charity Worker 2	Should we be expecting him to join us?
Scrooge	*We* will expect nothing, sir, least of all the presence of Jacob Marley, for he has been dead these past seven years. In fact, he died seven years ago on this very night.

The clock chimes for seven o'clock. Cratchit slowly gets himself ready to go home throughout the following exchange.

Charity Worker 1	Well, I am certainly sorry to hear that, sir. May his soul rest in peace.

The fire blazes brightly in a flash, and everyone in Scrooge's office turns to face it. After a moment, they turn back.

Charity Worker 2	I trust that his good nature lives on in his surviving partner.
Scrooge	We are indeed of similar character, sir.
Charity Worker 1	Oh, very good sir!
Charity Worker 2	Yes, very good indeed!
Charity Worker 1	Mr Scrooge, at this time of year, there are a great many people throughout the city who suffer terribly.
Charity Worker 2	With little food or warmth, many people need the support of those who are in a position to help.

Charity Worker 1	It is for this reason we have come to you today.
Charity Worker 2	Many thousands are in want of common necessaries.
Charity Worker 1	Indeed, many thousands more are in want of basic comforts. It is our wish that you may offer them a little hope at this most difficult time.

*They stand looking hopefully at **Scrooge**. **Scrooge** stares back at them, unaffected.*

Charity Worker 1	So, what should we put you down for?
Scrooge	Nothing.
Charity Worker 2	You wish to remain anonymous?
Scrooge	I wish to be left alone.
Charity Worker 1	Mr Scrooge?
Scrooge	Are there no prisons?
Charity Worker 2	Mr Scrooge?
Scrooge	And the workhouses, are they still in operation?
Charity Worker 1	They are, sir, regrettably so.
Scrooge	Ah, from your pitiful appeal I assumed that the usual haunts for the poor and lowly had all but disappeared.
Charity Worker 2	Mr Scrooge, you are one of the fortunate few who are in a position to help those who struggle every day just to maintain the most basic existence.
Charity Worker 1	The cold and hunger affect many thousands of people, and you really should—

*Throughout this exchange **Scrooge** rises and begins to force the **Charity Workers** towards the exit.*

Scrooge	I really should mind my own business, sir, as should you. You ask that I, a man who has worked his whole life to attain a fortune, such as it is, would give to those who cannot be

bothered to work a full day for an honest man's pay. The prisons and workhouses offer the basic necessities that you ask for, and it is my taxes that cover that particular expense. Therefore, sir, I have given all I am willing to give, and indeed, all I should be expected to give.

Charity Worker 2 Mr Scrooge, many would rather die than go to the workhouses.

Scrooge If they would rather die, may they do it, and decrease the surplus population. Good day to you, gentlemen.

Scrooge slams the door behind him. As soon as the door is slammed shut, it knocks again. Scrooge yells with frustration and opens it.

Scrooge I told you to leave me in peace!

Scrooge sees that it is a young boy standing holding his hat out. The Boy starts singing O Holy Night.

Carol-singing Boy *[Singing]* O holy night! The stars are brightly shining,
It is the night of our dear Saviour's birth.
Long lay the world in sin and error pining,
Till He appeared and the soul felt its worth.
A thrill of hope the weary world rejoices,
For yonder breaks a new and glorious morn.
Fall on your knees! O, hear the angel voices!
O night divine, O night when Christ was born;
O night divine, O night, O night divine!

There is a moment where Scrooge almost seems moved, before he turns the Boy around and kicks his backside to send him on his way. As he turns, Cratchit is stood in his coat and scarf, waiting to be given permission to go home. Scrooge looks rather annoyed at the expectant and hopeful expression on his face.

Scrooge And I suppose you will be expecting the full day tomorrow?

Cratchit It *is* Christmas, sir.

Scrooge	That may be so, Cratchit, but it is a poor excuse to expect an employer to pay a day's wages to an absent employee.
Cratchit	It is only once a year, Mr Scrooge.
Scrooge	Which makes it no better, Cratchit. If you expect a day off tomorrow, I shall expect you all the earlier the following day.

Scrooge takes out a large sack of coins. Cratchit's face lights up at seeing such a huge amount of money. Scrooge holds it up, but before Cratchit can reach it, Scrooge takes a smaller bag out of it. Cratchit looks mildly disappointed, but still eager to get his wages. This Russian doll situation continues until Scrooge gets down to a tiny money bag. By this point Cratchit looks utterly dejected. Out of the bag, Scrooge lifts two coins and offers them to Cratchit. Cratchit takes them and holds them up to inspect them. Scrooge takes one of them back, and goes to reach for the other before Cratchit quickly pockets it.

Cratchit	Thank you, Mr Scrooge! And a very merry—

*Cratchit realizes the futility of wishing **Scrooge** a merry Christmas, and runs off in delight. **Scrooge** puts on his coat and hat, and blows out the remaining candle in his office.*

●●

SCENE 2

The streets of London, and Scrooge's apartment.

Marley *[Narrating]* Scrooge left the office that night, and walked his usual route back home. The streets were more crowded than usual with last-minute shoppers collecting Christmas puddings, choirs singing hymns on street corners, and by children playing in the snow. Scrooge hated it all, and was relieved when he finally got to his front door.

Scrooge fumbles in his pockets for his keys. He finds them, and as he reaches for the lock he drops them in shock. There, on his front door, is the face of Jacob Marley.

Scrooge Jacob Marley! But he's gone! I could have sworn I saw his face right here, but yet … oh come now, Ebenezer! Must have been a trick of the light, humbug the lot of it. You've been working yourself too hard, that must be it – the stress of working has made you see things that are not really there! Yes, that's it …

Marley *[Narrating]* Scrooge was shaken by this strange encounter. He was a practical man, one who was not inclined to believe in anything extraordinary or supernatural. However, Scrooge's reluctance to believe the evidence of his senses was about to be pushed to the limit …

Scrooge looks with great unease once more at both sides of the door, and enters. He potters about in his apartment, taking off his coat and hat, and getting into his nightgown and nightcap. He gets his bowl of gruel and sits before his fire.

Scrooge   Ha! Jacob Marley! If he could have seen me before he would have laughed! What a humbug, the lot of it!

*The sound of the **Carol Singers** singing* Silent Night *in the distance is heard.*

Carol Singers   Silent night, holy night
All is calm, all is bright
Round yon Virgin Mother and Child
Holy Infant so tender and mild
Sleep in heavenly peace
Sleep in heavenly peace.

Scrooge goes to his window.

Scrooge   Get out of it you noisy brutes! If you preach a silent night, it's a wonder you don't give us a silent night!

He goes again to his chair in front of the fire.

The sooner this menace of a season is over, the sooner there shall be order once more on the streets. And that, more than anything else, will be cause for celebration. Maybe even I shall sing then! Ha!

A bell gently rings in Scrooge's home. At first he cannot locate the source of the noise, but as he finds it, a second bell starts to ring, and then a third, until a cacophony of noise dominates Scrooge's apartment.

What the devil is going on? What is this?

The lights go out suddenly. The noise stops. A clanking noise replaces it, footsteps approaching, and the sound of heavy chains rattling. Scrooge whimpers in the dark.

What's going on? Hello? Is there anyone there? Show yourselves!

The ghost of Jacob Marley enters. He is weighed down by thick, heavy chains. He stares into the eyes of Scrooge.

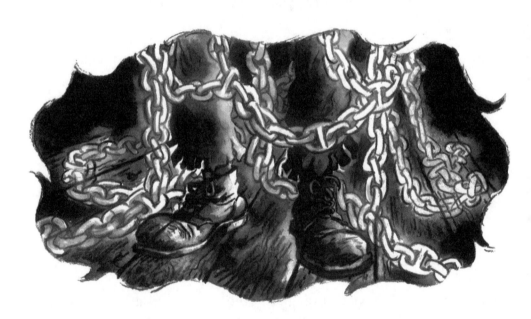

	This … I mean … well it's obviously … I … I don't believe it.
Marley	Scrooge …
Scrooge	I can't believe it … I won't believe it … I—
Marley	Ebenezer Scrooge …
Scrooge	Speak not my name for I will not hear it! Not from you, for you are not real! You cannot exist if I refuse to believe what I see!

Marley	You do believe.
Scrooge	I do not! I've read about things like this. Apparitions brought on by stress or … or food poisoning! How do I know you are not just an undigested bit of beef, or an old potato?

Marley stares at Scrooge.

Marley	Do I look like a potato?
Scrooge	Well …

Marley raises his arms in the air, and the bells chime louder than before, the fire burns brighter than before, and the lights rapidly flicker on and off. Scrooge screams and cowers.

Stop! Please stop! I believe, I believe!

Everything stops.

But Jacob … I spoke your name today … two men in the office, and I … I said you died seven years ago today … seven years, has it really been that long? I … I …

Marley	Ebenezer Scrooge …
Scrooge	Jacob Marley … is it really you?

Marley nods.

But … you're supposed to be dead.

Marley	I am dead.
Scrooge	But … I don't understand … how … why … what … I mean … can you sit down?
Marley	I can.
Scrooge	Well … do it then.

Scrooge watches Marley sit and follows suit. They stare at each other, Marley certainly looking the more relaxed of the two. Scrooge looks very uncomfortable.

What … what do you want with me, Jacob Marley?

Marley	I have come from the great beyond with a warning for you. I have come to you before it is too late.
Scrooge	I … I don't understand.
Marley	These past seven years, I have watched you closely Scrooge, closer than you can imagine. I see how you are set in your ways, and how you are set upon your path.
Scrooge	Watched? Jacob … you're dead.
Marley	My spirit has wandered restlessly, relentlessly, within the four walls of our old counting house. I have seen your dealings with people, and I have watched you continue along your path, blindly. I have sat many a time, Ebenezer, over your shoulder. I have silently implored you to see the error of your ways, before it is too late.
Scrooge	Too late? Jacob, I don't—
Marley	In life I was much like you. I amassed a great fortune, and a great many enemies.
Scrooge	But you were always a good man of business, Jacob …
Marley	Business! Mankind was my business. The common welfare was my business; charity, kindness, mercy, and compassion, were all my business. The dealings of my trade were but a drop of water in the comprehensive ocean of my business!

Scrooge stares at him, dumbfounded.

Scrooge	What are you saying, Jacob?
Marley	When I died, seven years ago tonight, I found out to my horror that it is not enough to be successful in business, for it is our dealings with people that are most important.
Scrooge	Nonsense, Jacob! What is this you're saying? Why do you talk like this?
Marley	I mean to save you, Ebenezer. The chains I wear are the chains I forged in life, link by link, yard by yard. They weigh heavy on me, as they shall on you.

Scrooge	On me?
Marley	Your chains were as thick and as heavy as these seven Christmases ago, and you have continued in the same spirit ever since. It is these chains I wish to save you from.
Scrooge	Humbug! I refuse to believe it! You are not really here! You are not Jacob Marley! The Marley I knew would not have entertained such notions.
Marley	Listen to me, for my time here grows short. I seek to help you avoid a most terrible fate.
Scrooge	You were always a good friend, Jacob. Please, I beg you to—
Marley	Tonight you will be visited by three spirits.
Scrooge	I— I think I'd rather not …
Marley	Without them you cannot hope to avoid the road you are currently heading down. Expect the first when the clock strikes one.
Scrooge	One? That's awfully late, Jacob …
Marley	Expect the second when the clock strikes two.
Scrooge	Two?
Marley	And expect the third when the clock strikes …
Scrooge	Three?
Marley	Yes … three.
	Marley begins to exit.
Scrooge	Please, Marley, speak words of comfort to me. Tell me there's an easier way!
Marley	There is no other way.
Scrooge	Well, couldn't they all arrive at once and be done with it?
Marley	This is your only chance, Scrooge. Remember, the first spirit shall arrive at one.

Marley is gone. Scrooge is left alone on the stage. He goes to bed.

Scrooge   Jacob Marley … I … I dare not say it did not happen, yet how could it be? Jacob Marley indeed! He's dead, Ebenezer, you old fool! Three spirits … no, no that cannot be! Can it? Enough! I should not dwell on it too much, for such a thing would interrupt my sleep tonight. To bed … yes, to bed.

Scrooge goes towards his bed, then turns to pick up a poker from beside the fireplace. He goes to bed with the poker, and looks very nervous. He looks around, then closes the bed curtains.

● ●

SCENE 3

Scrooge's apartment; a country lane; an old schoolhouse; Mr Fezziwig's office; another office.

After a short time a bell tolls once. Scrooge jumps out from his bed, looking all around. He sees nothing.

Scrooge	Enough! Gather yourself, Scrooge, for goodness sake! You're shaking like a leaf, and for what? Three spirits? Well, let them come if they will. I will not give them occasion to trouble me!
	*Scrooge turns towards his bed to see that a figure has appeared. It is the **Ghost of Christmas Past**.*
	AAAAARRRRRGGGGHHHH! HELP! SWEET MOTHER OF MERCY, HELP ME!
	Scrooge lifts the poker like a sword.
	Are you the spirit whom Jacob Marley warned me of?
Past	I am.
	Scrooge realizes how silly he looks, and lowers the poker.
Scrooge	Who ... what are you?
Past	I am the Ghost of Christmas Past. Your Christmases past.
Scrooge	You need not have come, spirit. I have no wish to revisit my past.
	*The **spirit** looks at him.*
	What do you want from me?
Past	I want nothing of you. I ask nothing of you.
Scrooge	And I require nothing from you! Therefore, you've had a wasted journey!
Past	Our journey has not yet begun.
Scrooge	Our journey? I was told that I would be visited by three spirits! I was not informed that I would be required to make any journey. No, this simply will not do! I demand that you leave at once!
Past	Ebby.
Scrooge	This is my property and I ... what did you call me?
	*The **spirit** smiles at **Scrooge**.*
	Spirit, the weather, the hour, and least of all, my dressing gown are not adapted to pedestrian ... or other purposes.

*The **spirit**'s hand is outstretched. She smiles. **Scrooge** tentatively takes the **spirit**'s hand.*

***Scrooge** and the **spirit** find themselves in a country lane.*

I know this place. This is where I grew up! This is the very lane in which the boys used to play cricket.

Past	You played cricket?
Scrooge	Well, not really. I mean, school is for learning, academia. I was a scholar; I excelled at Latin, at Mathematics. I was here to learn, not to play …
Past	You would have liked to have played.
Scrooge	I would not … I … well, perhaps.

A boy walks by them, as if they were not there.

Look, that boy was in my dormitory! Joseph! Joseph Wiggins! Joseph!

Past	He cannot hear you.
Scrooge	What are you talking about? He's standing but five feet from me! Joseph Wiggins!
Past	He cannot hear you. We are but shadows in your past. Not a soul will see or hear you. We are here only to observe, not to communicate. Now come with me.
Scrooge	Where are we going?

*The **spirit** looks away from **Scrooge**.*

Scrooge	Ah! The schoolhouse. Yes, that was more my dwelling. My place of study and I excelled at it. I was always told so.
Past	You were happy?
Scrooge	Happy? Yes … yes, of course I was happy.
Past	I see a shadow of a boy, alone and crying in the schoolroom at Christmas. He is far from his home, and from his sister, while his classmates returned home to make merry with family.

*Young Scrooge enters the stage and sits at his desk. He cries. **Old Scrooge** approaches him, and is clearly moved.*

Scrooge	Yes, I suppose that … perhaps I was not as happy as I would have wished.
Past	You must see that boy.
Scrooge	I do not wish to see him! I—

Scrooge cries.

Past	Why do you cry?
Scrooge	He's just a boy. I was just a boy. I wish … but, no, it is too late now.
Past	What is it?
Scrooge	There was a lad at my office last night, singing a carol. I wish I had given him something, that's all.

*Scrooge looks again at **Young Scrooge**, and turns to leave.*

*Fan comes running into the schoolroom. **Young Scrooge** sees her and rises, embracing his sister.*

Fan	Ebby!

*Scrooge turns and sees **Fan**.*

Young Scrooge	Fan! What are you doing here?
Fan	Oh, Ebby! I have the most wonderful news!
Young Scrooge	What is it, Fan? What?
Fan	It's father! Oh, Ebby, I don't think you'd believe it unless you saw it for yourself! He's changed; it's all different now at home. I've come to bring you back!
Young Scrooge	What? How … I … I don't understand!
Fan	He's kinder now, gentler. He doesn't get cross any more, and two nights ago he was tucking me into bed, and I took a chance and asked if you could come home for Christmas, and he said, 'Yes'!

SCENE 3   ACT 1

31

Young Scrooge	What?
Fan	Yes! He even arranged for me to come in a carriage and collect you. Oh, my darling brother, we're going to have the most splendid Christmas this year! Quickly, come now! Get your things! It's time to come home.

*They embrace once more, then run off excitedly, leaving **Scrooge** and the **Ghost of Christmas Past** alone.*

Past	Did this not prove to be a happy Christmas for you?
Scrooge	Happy? Well … yes. Yes, it was.
Past	You look happy.
Scrooge	My dear Fan, my beautiful sister. She was a wonderful girl.
Past	She was your only sister?
Scrooge	Yes.
Past	She is dead now?
Scrooge	Yes.
Past	She had a son, did she not? Your nephew?
Scrooge	Fred. It is only now I see her in him. How did I not see it before?
Past	It is time for you to see another Christmas, Ebby.
Scrooge	Please, spirit! That name is no longer … my name is—

*The **spirit**'s voice is now different.*

Past	Ebenezer Scrooge!
Scrooge	Spirit? I recognize that voice … it's—
Past	Ebenezer Scrooge!

*Scrooge and the **spirit** find themselves at the office of Mr Fezziwig.*

*A Christmas party is in full swing. **Mr Fezziwig** is talking enthusiastically with party guests.*

Scrooge	Look! It's old Fezziwig, my old boss. He looks exactly as I remember him!
Mr Fezziwig	Ebenezer Scrooge!
	Young Scrooge comes rushing in clutching papers.
Old and Young Scrooge	Yes Mr Fezziwig!
Mr Fezziwig	If you don't put down that work this instant—
Young Scrooge	Mr Fezziwig, sir, I have noticed an irregularity in one of the accounts.
Mr Fezziwig	Really? Should I be concerned?
Young Scrooge	Well, sir, in the last year, due to an oversight on our part, Mr McGregor's account is in debt to us by a total of nine pence.
Mr Fezziwig	Good Lord! Mr Scrooge, run out this instant and fetch me the Bow Street Runners! *
	Young Scrooge turns on his heels and runs as Mr Fezziwig breaks into laughter.
Scrooge	Ha ha! Old Fezziwig, he was fantastic! He could have you laughing one minute and crying the next! Look at me! I was rather wet behind the ears.
	Young Scrooge runs back to Mr Fezziwig.
Young Scrooge	Mr Fezziwig, you're mocking me, aren't you?
Mr Fezziwig	Oh come along now, Mr Scrooge. Your devotion to me and this company is a delightful thing to see. You are a loyal employee and a good friend and tonight we are celebrating that! That is what Christmas is all about. Put down those papers and come and join me!
	Young Scrooge smiles.
Young Scrooge	Very well, Mr Fezziwig.

---

* The Bow Street Runners were recognized as London's first police force.

Young Scrooge puts down the paperwork and notices a young lady talking to some other guests. Young Scrooge approaches Mr Fezziwig, who is talking now with Mrs Fezziwig.

Young Scrooge	Mr Fezziwig, who is that lady?
Mr Fezziwig	Oh, this is Mrs Fezziwig. Darling, this is Mr Scrooge. I've told you about him haven't I?
Mrs Fezziwig	Oh, yes you have. It is a pleasure to meet you, Mr Scrooge. Mr Fezziwig has told me a lot about you. Quite a bright future ahead of you if I am to believe everything I am told!
Young Scrooge	Well I'm not sure about …
Mr Fezziwig	Nonsense, Ebenezer. You are a bright young man and that's for sure!
Young Scrooge	Thank you Mr Fezziwig. It is a pleasure to meet you Mrs Fezziwig.
Mrs Fezziwig	And now, what about Belle Winklesworth?

Young Scrooge looks confused.

That is the name of the young lady you were enquiring about.

Young Scrooge	Oh no, no you misunderstand. I wasn't … I was just … Miss Winklesworth, you say?
Mr Fezziwig	That's right. Why don't you go over and introduce yourself? She could do a lot worse than you!
Young Scrooge	Oh no, I couldn't. I mean … what would I say?
Mrs Fezziwig	Just say 'Hello'! She is a lovely girl.
Mr Fezziwig	Yes, go on lad. Why not, eh?
Young Scrooge	Yes, you're right. Why not? I'll go over and I'll say, 'Good evening, I'm Mr Scrooge', or should I say 'Ebenezer'? I'll say 'Ebenezer', and when I do I shall kiss her hand . . . but then she might take offence and scream! Mr Fezziwig, what do I do if she screams?
Mrs Fezziwig	Good heavens … he's mad.

*Mr Fezziwig takes **Young Scrooge** by the arm and drags him towards **Belle**.*

Mr Fezziwig	Miss Winklesworth, Mr Scrooge!

Young Scrooge and Belle greet each other and begin to dance together during the following exchange.

Scrooge	Spirit, I no longer wish to be here.
Past	What is it about this woman that has brought about such a sudden change?
Scrooge	That is my business and my business alone! I wish to leave!
Past	This is a happy time for you, is it not?
Scrooge	Happy? Ha! That's an understatement; this was the happiest night of my life. Look at her.
Past	What happened?
Scrooge	Do you delight, spirit, in making me relive this pain? Is that your true purpose tonight? Am I being punished? To see her again is both thrilling and painful in equal measure. If you wish to punish me consider it done.
Past	I am not here to punish you. I wish to help you. What happened?
Scrooge	After a short time we were engaged, but … nothing has ever gone right for me! I loved her and she left!
Past	And why did she leave?
Scrooge	Enough! I cannot watch this any longer.
Past	We have one more visit to make before we finish, and then I must leave you.
Scrooge	What?
Past	*[In a changed voice]* Goodbye, Ebenezer.
Scrooge	Spirit, I—

*Scrooge and the **spirit** find themselves in an office.*

*Young Scrooge is sitting at his desk counting his money. He barely pays attention to **Belle**.*

Belle	Goodbye, Ebenezer.
Scrooge	Very well, I shall see you tonight.
Belle	No, you do not understand. I came to tell you that—
Young Scrooge	Can this not wait, Belle? I have Mr Marley arriving at any moment, and it's a very important meeting. Mr Marley is of a certain character, and—
Belle	This cannot wait.
Young Scrooge	Of course it can. I have business in the office today, and—
Belle	And tomorrow, and the next day.

Young Scrooge finally looks up.

Young Scrooge	What are you talking about? Without the business we would have no money! Would you prefer to be poor?
Belle	I would have preferred us to be happy. Are you happy, Ebenezer? Truly happy?
Young Scrooge	Are you not? You must understand that this is an important time in my business, Belle. I have to make small sacrifices or the business shall suffer.
Belle	Small sacrifices? I do not recognize you any more. You have become so blinded to anything that does not yield you a profit.
Young Scrooge	What are you talking about?
Belle	Tell me, Ebenezer, if you had your life over, if you could go back, knowing then what you know now, would you choose a dowerless* girl? One who could offer you no gain?

Silence.

Scrooge	Yes, I would.

---

* Without a dowry; a dowry is a sum of money or property paid by the bride's family to her husband. Dowries were common among the upper-classes in Victorian England.

Young Scrooge	You think not.
Belle	I would gladly think otherwise, if I could. I hope the mistress who has replaced me makes you happy, Ebenezer.

Young Scrooge	Mistress? Belle, have you gone mad? There's no one but you!
	Young Scrooge stands, and in doing so knocks coins onto the floor. He bends to pick them up.
Belle	That used to be true; now there is only one love in your life.
Scrooge	I was trying to build a business …
Belle	And I will never be as important as her.
Scrooge	I wanted the best for you.
Belle	And so, I release you, Ebenezer, with a full heart for the love of him you once were.
Scrooge	Stop her, you fool!
	*Belle exits. **Young Scrooge** turns and returns to his desk. **Scrooge** stares at **Young Scrooge**.*
	You will find yourself quite alone in the world …
Past	Come home, Ebenezer.
	Scrooge finds himself in his bed again, alone.

SCENE 4

Scrooge's apartment; Cratchit's home; Fred's home; a deserted place.

Scrooge *lets out a whimper, but quickly gathers himself before looking at the clock. It is approaching two o'clock.*

Scrooge	Almost two. No sooner am I rid of one spirit than another shall be inflicted upon me.

The clock chimes for two o'clock. **Scrooge** *looks out of his bed, and once again cannot see anything. He hears merry laughter from somewhere. He gets up to locate the source of the laughter, and as he gets closer, the* **Ghost of Christmas Present** *bursts in with a large bottle in one hand. His appearance is truly merry.*

He walks past **Scrooge** *to one of the chairs by the fireplace.* **Scrooge** *stays still, staring at the ghost.*

Present	Come in! Come in, and know me better man.
Scrooge	What are you?
Present	Forgive me, I was under the impression Jacob Marley told you I'd be along.

Scrooge	Well, he did … I mean, he said … well, I just don't really … that is to say that—
Present	What do I look like?
Scrooge	What do you look like? I'm not quite sure …
Present	I should think you have never seen the like of me before, eh?
Scrooge	No, never.
Present	I am the Ghost of Christmas Present.
Scrooge	My Christmas present?
Present	Yes, your Christmas present, Scrooge.
Scrooge	I … I don't much care for Christmas.
Present	Yes I know, you have ignored my brothers for many years now.
Scrooge	Your brothers?
Present	Yes, the spirits of Christmas. They are all my brothers, more than eighteen hundred. Your life has seen but a few of these and you have turned your back on them all. But you shall not turn your back on me.
Scrooge	What would you have with me, spirit?
Present	I would have you see Christmas, Scrooge, nothing more than that.

Scrooge seems unable to meet his gaze.

Are you scared of me?

Scrooge	Scared? No …
Present	You need not fear me, Scrooge. I am here to help you. You must look upon me, and allow yourself to enjoy it! Look at me!

Scrooge hesitantly looks at him.

Am I so awful to look upon?

Scrooge	Well . . . no.

Present	In fact, I'm rather nice to look at, am I not?

*Scrooge looks at the **spirit** and allows a giggle.*

Scrooge	Well, I suppose …

*The **spirit** hands **Scrooge** the bottle.*

Present	Drink this.
Scrooge	What is it?
Present	Just drink it!

Scrooge sniffs it, then takes a hesitant sip. His face lights up.

Ha! You like it?

Scrooge	It's magnificent! What is it?
Present	Never you mind, old family recipe. It cannot fail to get even the most reluctant of souls into the festive spirit.

Scrooge takes a gulp. His spirits are visibly lifting.

Steady now, I need you sober enough to take in what I have to show you!

Scrooge	What is it you wish to show me, spirit?
Present	Your fellow man, Ebenezer. I wish for you to see how the people who surround you every day manage to overcome the misery you positively radiate, and manage to have themselves a merry Christmas.
Scrooge	I will go with you, spirit. I will go with you and your delicious mystery drink!

Scrooge takes another gulp.

*Scrooge and the **spirit** find themselves outside the home of **Bob Cratchit**.*

Where are we?

*There is silence. **Scrooge** looks around for a moment before **Mrs Cratchit** bursts in, shouting.*

*The following passage is delivered whilst the family talk over each other and make preparations for Christmas dinner. It is hectic, and **Scrooge** and the **spirit** move around the family while they make their preparations.*

Mrs Cratchit   Careful now! Gravy coming through! It's piping hot! Watch now, Tim, stay out of my way! Robert? You haven't set a place for Martha! Where is she? She's fifteen minutes late. Good heavens, Tim, put away your toys now and wash your hands. Robert! Quickly, we need to get the table sorted; the bird will be ready any moment. Tim, was that the door? Check to see if it is your sister. Robert, is that a potato you were pinching? Serves you right, they're just out of the oven! Not those plates, Robert, the nice ones. Tim! Was that Martha at the door? Tell her I could use her help. Goodness, the carrots! I forgot about those! Tim?

Cratchit   Giddyup there, horsie! What a stallion, Timothy! Watch out, son, do keep out of Mother's way with him though. Martha! Of course, I'll grab some more cutlery! Your mother's right, son, wash those hands; you've been handling horses all day! Quickly son! I'll be one moment, Emily, just washing a fork for Martha! Oh! It's burnt my mouth! Will these plates do? We only have three nice ones; never mind, I'll have a cast one. Tim! The door! There's my girl! Martha, Merry Christmas my love!

Tim   Father, what do horses eat? What will my horsie have for dinner? Sorry, Mother. Father, could Bobby eat gravy? Will I have to walk him? Will you walk him with me? Could we paint Bobby? Yes, Mother. Come along, Bobby, we must wash up before dinner. The door? Yes, Mother, I'm just finishing washing up. I'm coming! Martha! Merry Christmas! Mother! Father! Martha is here! She's brought a present! Who is that for? Is it for me? Oh, it's for Mother. That's nice. Look, I got a horse! He's called Bobby!

Martha   *[After she arrives]* Hello Tim! Merry Christmas! Sorry I'm late. Where is Mother? No, it's not for you, it's a present for all of us. Well, you'll just have to wait and see! Merry Christmas, Father! Merry Christmas, Mother!

*As preparations reach their conclusion, **Cratchit** takes a glass and taps it with his fork.*

Cratchit	Ladies and gentlemen, if you would care to make your way to the table, the Cratchit family feast is about to begin.

*The **Cratchits** gather around the table.*

Now, my loves. Are we all comfortable? Well then, let me be the first to say—

***Cratchit** gasps. The children look confused.*

Oh no! Emily!

Mrs Cratchit	What is it, Robert?
Cratchit	Oh no, Emily, we've made a dreadful mistake!
Mrs Cratchit	Oh Robert, I think I know what you mean!
Tim	What is it?
Cratchit	Children, it is with great regret that I have to tell you your mother and I have forgotten to put the turkey in the oven.
Mrs Cratchit	We're so sorry, my darlings.
Martha	Don't worry Mother. We can do it tomorrow, instead.
Tim	Yes, although Father will be at work. Perhaps we could eat in the evening? Although … hold on! If you've forgotten to cook the turkey then what's that delicious smell?

They burst into laughter.

Cratchit	What a smart boy you are!
Mrs Cratchit	There's no fooling our Tim!
Martha	Oh Father! What a silly joke!

***Mrs Cratchit** brings in the tiny bird.*

Cratchit	It is with great delight we present to you, the bird!
	They cheer and laugh.
	Now children, watch as your father skilfully carves this juicy bird!
Mrs Cratchit	Robert! We will say grace first!
Cratchit	How absolutely right your mother is! Firstly children, we thank God for giving us this time together. And, we give thanks to your mother for putting together such a delicious feast. Not just today, but every day she does it, for God knows I can't cook!
	They laugh.
Mrs Cratchit	Nonsense Robert! Furthermore, we would like to say our thanks to you for working so hard and providing for your family.
	*The children agree, and **Cratchit** leans over to kiss her.*
Martha	Well, I would like to thank you both. I would also like to thank Mr Davis, the baker, and my boss, who is good to me all year round, *and* has provided us with a lovely loaf of bread for today!
Mrs Cratchit	That was very kind of him, Martha, but you do work hard for him!

| Tim | I especially want to say thank you for Bobby here! He'll be my best friend! Maybe next Christmas I could get another horsie for him to run around with? |

*Tim focuses on his wooden horse, and this is followed by a brief silence as **Mrs Cratchit** and **Martha** look at **Tim**, then to **Bob**.*

| Cratchit | Yes, Tim … why not? Next Christmas … another friend for Bobby. |

| Mrs Cratchit | Robert, darling, you've forgotten the carving knife. |

Cratchit looks at her.

| | The knife, Bob. You run and fetch it. |

| Cratchit | Of course. I won't do much carving without my carving knife, will I? |

*He leaves to get the knife. **Scrooge** moves forward towards **Tim**.*

| Scrooge | Spirit, the boy … will he live? |

| Present | I see an image of an empty chair in his place next Christmas, and a crutch without an owner. |

| Scrooge | Don't say that, spirit! Do not say such a thing! There must be something that can be done? |

Cratchit re-enters.

| Cratchit | Here we go! Now, before we tuck into this delicious feast, there is one more person left to thank. I would like to thank the founder of this feast, Mr Ebenezer Scrooge. |

| Mrs Cratchit | Robert! |

| Cratchit | Emily, it's only right that we should thank him. After all, it is Mr Scrooge that pays my wage. |

| Mrs Cratchit | If you could call it a wage! Not so much as a penny's raise in six years! No, I'm sorry Robert, I will not give thanks to Mr Scrooge for he doesn't deserve it. |

Silence.

Cratchit	Emily, I know Mr Scrooge has a reputation for being somewhat uncharitable, but—
Mrs Cratchit	Uncharitable? He's as tight as a dead man's fist!
Cratchit	Emily, please! The children …
Mrs Cratchit	The children indeed! They suffer as we do from his cold-heartedness!
	More silence. **Scrooge** *looks affected by this discussion, and after a moment, begins to move away. When* **Tim** *speaks, he stops and turns back.*
Tim	I will drink his health for Father's sake, and I'll save a prayer for Mr Scrooge.
Mrs Cratchit	A prayer for Mr Scrooge, love?
Tim	He always looks so sad … God bless him. God bless everyone.
	Cratchit *applauds these words, and* **Mrs Cratchit** *looks lovingly at her son and at her husband. She raises her glass.*
Mrs Cratchit	To Mr Scrooge.
	The **Cratchits** *commence their feast.* **Scrooge** *stands and watches them, clearly moved. After a moment, the* **spirit** *approaches* **Scrooge**.
Present	Come, Ebenezer. We have one more stop to make.
	Scrooge *reluctantly leaves.* **Scrooge** *and the* **spirit** *find themselves at* **Fred's**, *where there is a party in full swing. People are drinking and talking and laughing. The* **Ghost of Christmas Present** *watches as* **Scrooge** *walks amongst the guests, and almost against his will, gets drawn into the spirit of the party.* **Scrooge** *swigs merrily from the bottle the* **spirit** *gave him.*
Fred	Come on, Lizzy, you have one more question!
Elizabeth	Oh, I don't know! Let me see … it's large, it's round, it's orange and it's not a living thing?
Party Guest 1	No, it's not living. What is it?

Elizabeth	It's … I don't know … a very large orange?
	They all laugh.
Fred	No! It's the sun!
Elizabeth	The sun? Oh well, I would never have guessed that! Whose turn is it next?
Party Guest 2	I've got one here for Fred!
	*Party Guest 2 grabs a bit of paper. They laugh. Other guests look at the piece of paper and laugh as they see it. They whisper to each other, and now everyone except **Fred** seems to be in on the joke.*
Party Guest 2	Alright, off you go! Ten questions!
Scrooge	I say, spirit, I'm rather enjoying myself! I bet I'll get this before he does!
Fred	Okay! Is it a living thing?
Party Guest 3	Barely living!
	The guests laugh.
Fred	Barely living? Food maybe? Is it a fruit?
Party Guest 1	No!
Fred	A vegetable?
Party Guest 2	No! Not a vegetable!
Fred	An animal?
Party Guest 2	Oh, it's certainly a beast!
	*Party Guest 2 shows the paper to **Party Guest 1**, who laughs.*
Fred	Right! A dangerous animal … does it have claws?
Party Guest 2	I believe so.
Fred	Does it roar?
Party Guest 2	Oh, it's been known to roar!
Fred	I say it's … a lion!

Party Guest 2	Wrong!
Scrooge	I knew it! It's a bear! I tell you, spirit, it's a bear!
Party Guest 2	Come along Fred, a nasty animal—
Party Guest 1	It's mean and known to roar …
Fred	I give up! What is it?
Party Guest 3	Your Uncle Ebenezer!

*They laugh heartily; **Scrooge** looks dejected. He walks away from the circle.*

Fred	Very good, very good! But come now, he's not as bad as all that!
Party Guest 1	Although I say Fred should get half a point, he is as fierce as a lion!

More laughter from the guests.

Fred	Oh stop it, now! I know we get plenty of merriment out of him, but the truth is I feel sorry for him. I couldn't be angry with him if I tried. Who suffers most by his ill whims? He does, always. Yet it is Christmas, and it is only right that we wish him good health and a merry Christmas. He wouldn't take it from me, but I wish it to him nonetheless.

The party guests raise their glasses.

All	To Scrooge!

*Scrooge looks taken aback by **Fred**'s sentiments, and approaches him as if he would like to say something, but realizes that it would be useless to do such a thing. As everyone at the party goes back to talking amongst themselves, the **Ghost of Christmas Present** approaches **Scrooge** and touches him on the shoulder.*

Present	We must go, Scrooge.
Scrooge	I'm … yes, let's go.

*Scrooge and the **spirit** find themselves in a dark and shadowy place. The **spirit** appears weary and frail. He sits on a nearby* *mound and rests.* **Scrooge** *approaches him and offers him the bottle, which the* **spirit** *accepts.*

Present	Goodness, what a change! Ebenezer Scrooge giving to someone else!
Scrooge	I feel changed, spirit. What now? What do we see here?

The **spirit** *looks at him and smiles.*

Present	My time is near an end. I must leave you now.
Scrooge	You're leaving? No, spirit! I daresay I have enjoyed your company, something I haven't felt in many years.
Present	Then I have done you some good.
Scrooge	You have!

Two children appear behind **Scrooge***. Their faces are obscured. They are frail and dirty, and are clearly undernourished and unwell. They slowly walk hand in hand towards* **Scrooge***.* **Scrooge** *notices them.*

You there, boy! What has happened to your face?

The boy looks towards **Scrooge***. He doesn't answer.*

Are you alright? Is the girl your sister? What has happened to your face?

Present	They are the faces of many thousands of children. They are the faces of Ignorance and Want.
Scrooge	Of who?
Present	The boy is Ignorance. The girl is Want. They, like many hundreds and thousands of others, are alone, frightened, and neglected.
Scrooge	I cannot see their eyes.
Present	No, you cannot see them. But you can feel them. They stare into your soul. But, you have chosen to close the door to your soul, and to your heart. And now you will not help them.

Scrooge *walks slowly towards the children.*

Present	Fear these children, Ebenezer. Fear them both, but mostly fear the boy, for I see doom written on his brow, unless that writing can be erased.
Scrooge	What? I … I don't know what … please, spirit. Stop this.
Present	I cannot stop this, Scrooge. Only you can change their fate.
Scrooge	Have they no home? No refuge to go to?
Present	Are there no prisons? No workhouses?
Scrooge	Spirit … I—

*Scrooge turns to face the children and moves towards them, slowly. The **spirit** watches him.*

You need not fear me, boy. Here, take my hand.

*Scrooge reaches out his hand to the boy, but as he almost reaches him, a loud scream or cry that is almost animalistic comes from the boy and shocks **Scrooge**, who falls back. The children and the **spirit** disappear.*

Spirit! Wait! Come back! I need your help! I heed your lessons; I recognize the need to change! I can be better, but I need your help! Spirit!

*A bell chimes three times. The **Ghost of Christmas Future** appears at **Scrooge's** side. **Scrooge** gasps, then composes himself.*

Spirit?

*The **spirit** stares at **Scrooge** in silence.*

Spirit … I am in the presence of … are you the Spirit of Christmases Yet to Come? You will show me things that have not yet happened, is that so?

*The **spirit** nods once.*

Ghost of Christmas Future, I am scared. But you are here to help me; you are here to help me mend. Your purpose is to do me good, is it not? I want to live, to live to be another man, so I will bear your company with a thankful heart. Will you not speak to me?

*Silence. The **spirit** points towards the exit.*

Very well, then lead on.

***Scrooge** follows the hooded figure of the **spirit** offstage.*

ACT 2

• •

SCENE 1

The streets of London; a pawn shop; Cratchit's home; a graveyard.

Scrooge *tentatively follows the* **Ghost of Christmas Future** *onstage and looks around. Two* **Merchants** *walk on from the other side of the stage.*

Merchant 1	They say the Thames has frozen over.
Merchant 2	Has been for two days.

*Merchant 3 enters, walking past **Scrooge** and the **spirit**.*

Merchant 3	Good afternoon, gentlemen.
Merchant 1	Good afternoon.
Merchant 2	News?
Merchant 3	Not much at all, except that it was some time last night.
Merchant 1	What was it that finally killed him?
Merchant 3	I don't really know all of the details. I just know that he's gone. He's dead.
Merchant 2	Really? Well! Do you know when he died?
Merchant 1	I believe it was some time last night.
Merchant 2	If I'm honest, I thought he'd never die!

They laugh.

Merchant 1	God knows what it was that finished him. What does it matter so long as something did!
Merchant 2	What did he do with all of his money?
Merchant 1	Who knows! He didn't leave it all to me, that's for sure!

They laugh.

Merchant 3	Perhaps he left it to his company.
Merchant 1	There won't be much of a turnout for the funeral.
Merchant 2	No, you're right. There wasn't many that liked him at all.
Merchant 1	Not many? Upon my life I cannot think of anyone who truly liked the man.

They laugh.

Merchant 3	What do you say we make up a party and go along to the funeral!

They laugh.

Merchant 2	I'll go if they provide a lunch!

They laugh raucously.

Merchant 1	Well, I must press on. All the best, then.

They exit.

Scrooge	What do you show me this for, spirit?

*The **spirit** stares at **Scrooge**. He points to the stage, where someone is setting up a washing line. Old rags hang from it. Under it is a smouldering fire. A man warms himself beside it.*

I don't understand, spirit, how did these people bear on my life? In my future, do I associate with such people?

***Scrooge** looks around, and doesn't recognize the place.*

What … where are we?

Old Joe	Come in, come in! Don't dilly-dally by the door, woman.

***Mary** rushes in carrying a bundle of clothes. She throws it down.*

Mary	Well, well, well. What odds, old Joe? I believe every person has the right to take care of themselves, and God knows he always did!
Old Joe	True, true, no man more so.

Mary	Well? What are you waiting for? Take a look and tell me what you think. Don't be afeared. Who's the worse for the loss of a few things like these? Not a dead man, at any rate.
Old Joe	No, indeed.

Old Joe hesitates to open the bundle.

Mary	If he wanted to keep them after he was dead, he should have been better in his lifetime. If he was, he'd have had someone to see him through to his last days. Instead, he lay there … for days … gasping out his last. Alone, in the dark, by himself.
Old Joe	Never a truer word spoken, miss. It was the bed he made for himself. It was his judgement.
Mary	And as I see it, he was let off very lightly! Had it been me casting out the punishment, he'd have been dealt worse. Now come along, Joe! Open up that bundle, and tell me what you'll give for it.

Old Joe opens the bundle.

Old Joe	Some sheets, two towels, some clothes, two old silver spoons, a pair of sugar tongs, and a pair of boots. And what's this?
Mary	I took all the food he had left in the house.
Old Joe	And what's this it's all wrapped up in?
Mary	Why, them's his bed curtains!
Old Joe	You don't mean that you took them down, rings and all as he was lying dead?
Mary	Yes! I did! And why not?
Old Joe	That's callous; it's horrible! I can't believe someone could do something so dastardly and downright immoral! I love it!

They laugh.

And are these his sheets and blankets?

Mary	The very same. I imagine it will be warm where he is now!

Old Joe suddenly drops the bundle.

Old Joe   I hope he didn't die of anything catching!

Old Joe pretends to struggle for breath, and slumps onto his side staring blankly into space. Mary looks unsure as to whether or not it's a joke, before Old Joe jumps up laughing. They both cackle.

Mary   Worry not, Joe. I believe he died of a bad heart, and a cruel one at that. You turn your attentions to that shirt, there. A fine one, it is, not a hole in it. That one was the best that he had, and they only would have wasted it.

Old Joe   Wasted it?

Mary   They was going to bury him in it! But I slipped it off his old, cold bones. He can be buried in a cheaper one! He can't look any uglier than he did at any rate!

Mary mimics how Scrooge looked when dead, and they laugh once more. Mary and Old Joe root through the bundle. Scrooge turns to the spirit.

Scrooge   Spirit, it's a wonder they don't try to sell this poor unfortunate's body itself.

Old Joe throws a bag of money down.

Old Joe   He frightened away all in his life, so that we may profit in his death!

Mary laughs, and they clear the stage, cackling. They exit, leaving Scrooge alone with the spirit.

Scrooge   Spirit, I understand if I do not mend my ways I will follow in the steps of this unhappy dead man that they talk of. Merciful heavens, show me no more! Heaven, be merciful, if there be any that felt anything for this poor man, take me to them. Let me see some tenderness.

Scrooge and the spirit find themselves in the Cratchit family home.

Mrs Cratchit is knitting in her chair. Martha sits by her chair, staring at the floor.

Mrs Cratchit   The dim light hurts my eyes, makes them weak. I wouldn't show your father weak eyes. It must be near his time now?

Martha   It is past, Mother. But he has walked a little slower these past few nights.

Mrs Cratchit   I've known him … I have known him walk very fast with Tiny Tim upon his shoulders. Very fast, indeed.

Martha   So have I, Mother. Often.

Martha stands and holds her mother.

Mrs Cratchit   Well, he was very light to carry, was Tim. Your father loved him so much that I believe he was no burden to carry at all.

Cratchit enters looking drained, yet cheerful.

Cratchit   Well, well, look here! What do we have here?

Martha runs to her father.

Martha, my darling Martha! And my beautiful wife, look at this lovely work.

Cratchit lifts his wife's knitting.

Lovely, you'll be done well before Sunday.

Cratchit sits at the table, staring blankly at the knitting.

Mrs Cratchit You went today then, Robert?

Cratchit Yes, my dear. And I so wish you could have come, too. Father Green really has been so wonderful and kind to us and he always was to Tim as well. I think it would have done you good to see what a light and peaceful place it is, and how pretty. It's called Green Acres. But you will see it in good time. I promised Tim that we would walk there every Sunday, and—

Cratchit suddenly breaks down, weeping.

My little boy, my little boy …

The family gathers around him. Cratchit controls himself.

I saw young Fred, Mr Scrooge's nephew, in the town today. He knew nothing of our plight, but must have gathered something from my face. He asked me what the matter was. Do you know, when I told him he said, 'I'm heartily sorry for it, Bob, and heartily sorry for your good wife'. He's a very decent man, Fred. Only met him on a couple of occasions previously, but he is a genuinely good soul. He told me that if he could be of any service, in any way, then we should not hesitate to call, and he handed me his card … there's nothing he can do … for us. But the kind way he spoke to me, it felt as though he really knew our Tim, and felt our pain with us.

Cratchit looks at his family.

I mustn't complain, I have a beautiful wife, and a very loving family. And we were lucky to have had Tim in our lives, even if it was for all too short a time.

The family embrace each other.

Scrooge Can nothing be done? Is this what *must* be? Have I been so blind?

Scrooge begins to cry.

Spirit, the ice has melted from my heart, but in its place there is a blazing fire! Is this what must be? Is it?

Scrooge and the spirit find themselves alone in a dark place.

Now I know this place; this court, this path. They are familiar to me. My home is not far from here … please spirit, take me there and show me who I become. I am ready to see.

The spirit turns away from Scrooge and points.

Spirit, this is not the way … what would you have me see over here?

Scrooge and the spirit enter a graveyard.

The spirit points behind Scrooge, at a gravestone. Scrooge looks at the grave, then back at the spirit with fear in his eyes. The spirit walks towards Scrooge, forcing Scrooge to his knees before the grave.

Spirit, I understand. I know the man of whom they were speaking before. I know whose grave this is. It is mine. Please, spirit, tell me that these are but the shadows of things that *could* be! I need a second chance, please! I tell you spirit, give me occasion, and I *will* change course. I will change paths. I will change my life's course and I will avoid these dark events. I CAN CHANGE, SPIRIT! PLEASE!

*A figure rises from the grave behind **Scrooge**, takes hold of him, and pulls him under. Another actor, with **Scrooge**'s same costume, rises out, and a struggle between the figure and **Scrooge** ensues in the grave. (This gives the actor playing **Scrooge** time to quietly exit, and get to his bed for Scene 2.)*

• •

SCENE 2

Scrooge's apartment.

***Scrooge** jumps up suddenly in his bed, screaming. He is alone in his apartment. He pats himself all over as if to check that he is really there, and he checks his own pulse. His face lights up.*

Scrooge   AHHHH! I'm … I'm alive … I'm here now for real in the flesh! Everything is in its place, my bed curtains and my bedding, all still here. They didn't take them and sell them! The spirit showed me not what would be, but what *could* be! Those dreadful visions may yet be changed! Oh, how clever they are! And you too, Jacob Marley! I haven't forgotten about you! Can you hear me? I think you can! Well if you can, thank you. I promise you Jacob Marley, on my knees, I will live in the past, present and future! The spirits of all three shall strive within me! I say it on my knees, Jacob Marley, on my knees! It's not too late! It starts today!

He jumps out of bed and runs around the room, grabbing his slippers and dressing-gown.

It's not too late! How wonderful! I've never felt so alive! Ha ha! I'm as merry as a cricket! What to do? What do I do? I know, of course! Right, let's get to it!

He runs out of his apartment and a few seconds later a scream is heard offstage. He re-enters his flat.

I suppose that I should put some clothes on first – we don't want to shock anyone else now do we? What to wear? What to wear? My shirt! My best shirt. I'll not be buried in it after all, at least not today! You know, I don't recall ever having that shirt on at all! It is a lovely shirt!

As he walks to pick up the shirt, he sees a small boy running by the window.

Hello there! You, boy! What day is this?

Delivery Boy   Who? Me, sir?

Scrooge   Yes, you boy! Tell me, what day is it?

Delivery Boy   Why, it's Christmas Day of course.

Scrooge   Oh joy! I haven't missed it! Oh, those clever spirits. They managed to get it all done in one night – who would have believed it?

Delivery Boy   The spirits, sir? You want to stay clear of them, sir. My mum likes the gin; my dad calls it 'mother's ruin'.

Scrooge   Ah ha ha! No lad, not that sort of … never mind. Listen, do you know the butcher's shop on the high street?

Delivery Boy   Why, yes sir.

Scrooge   And is the big turkey still hanging in the window there?

Delivery Boy   What, you mean the one as big as me?

Scrooge   Oh, what a clever boy you are! Yes that's the one! Well, is it still there?

Delivery Boy   It is, sir.

Scrooge   Well boy, run to the butcher and tell him to come here at once with that bird. I want to buy it! Here, catch this coin boy! Come back with the butcher in fifteen minutes and I'll give you another coin. Come back in ten and I'll give you sixpence!

Delivery Boy   Yes sir, yes Mr …

Scrooge   Scrooge, boy, Mr Scrooge.

Delivery Boy   Yes, sir, Mr Scrooge!

*The **Delivery Boy** runs off.*

Scrooge   I like that boy. Such a clever young man!

Scrooge goes to the mirror to straighten his tie.

ACT 2   SCENE 2

Goodness Ebenezer, has it been that long since you've worn a smile that you've forgotten how to do it!

Scrooge tries to smile, but isn't entirely successful.

Well, I suppose that will have to do! My goodness, people won't recognize this face; I hardly recognize it! I shall have to reintroduce myself to everyone, ho ho!

He acts out a conversation, interacting with various props.

Why, hello! Ebenezer Scrooge at your service, m'lady. And may I say how fabulous you look this evening? May I be so bold as to ask for this dance?

Scrooge dances with his shirt.

I hope you don't mind my saying, but you seem a little tense. Too much starch on your collar perhaps? Ha ha! You know, I have a waistcoat I think you would really hit it off with, perhaps I could introduce you?

He puts the shirt down.

Don't slouch darling! What, you're tired? Oh, it's a cuff life! Ha ha ha!

At the end of this he falls down, laughing, and looks in his mirror.

Young Fred has probably never seen his old Uncle Ebenezer smile before. And Cratchit! Bob Cratchit. He'll have quite a shock, I'm sure! Well, no time like the present. Today is the first day of the rest of my life!

Scrooge leaves laughing and giggling.

• •

SCENE 3

Cratchit's home.

*The **Cratchits** enter and settle into their Christmas morning.*

Cratchit   And this one is for Tim! Merry Christmas, son.

Cratchit produces a small package.

Tim	For me? Thank you, Father!

Tim unwraps the package and takes out a small book and a little wooden horse.

Cratchit	You see? I told you that I had got you a horse! Not quite what you had in mind, I'm sure, but nonetheless.
Tim	He's lovely, Father. I shall call him Bobby!
Mrs Cratchit	Now, run along and wash up, Tim! Then you can help me with the dinner.
Tim	Yes, Mother.

Tim exits.

Mrs Cratchit	He seemed pleased with his horse! You did a fine job of it, Bob. Now, if only you can work some magic with the food I'll be pleased as punch!
Cratchit	No need, my love. You are the finest cook in London!

Tim runs back in.

Tim	And I'll second that!
Cratchit	Good lad!
Mrs Cratchit	Well … I make the best with what we have, is all. Have you washed up then? That was quick.
Tim	Not yet, I had to get the door. Father, there is a turkey at the door.
Cratchit	What are you talking about, Tim?
Tim	There's a boy with a turkey. He says he's to deliver it here.
Cratchit	Well, he must have the wrong address.
Mrs Cratchit	Maybe it's for them over the road? I'll go and ask if … AARGH!

*The **Delivery Boy** carrying the turkey comes into the house.*

Delivery Boy	Can I put this down? I feel I might not last much longer otherwise …
Mrs Cratchit	I'm sorry, my love. It's just that bird being so big, it gave me a fright! It's not for us, anyhow. It'll be for across the way, don't you think, Bob? Bob?
Cratchit	That's no turkey, it's a monster! And I'm sure the Turkleberrys couldn't have afforded such a fine bird, God love 'em. No, no, no, you must be in the wrong place entirely, lad.
Delivery Boy	Are you the Cratchits?

Cratchit and *Mrs Cratchit* look at each other, before looking again at the *Delivery Boy*.

Cratchit	Well … yes.
Delivery Boy	Then this is yours. I think that's what it says on the card …
Mrs Cratchit	He's right, love, look. The card says so! *[Reading]* 'To the Cratchits, A very merry Christmas to you'.

Cratchit takes the card.

Cratchit	Well I … I never. It's for us alright! And you know … I almost recognize this writing … it's not unlike …
Mrs Cratchit	Bob?

Cratchit	No, that's silly. It's not. It couldn't be.
Mrs Cratchit	Well, whoever it is that has sent us this, they didn't intend for us to stand around staring at it! Tim, help me with it into the oven and let's just pray that the oven will take it!
	They struggle off with the turkey.

● ●

SCENE 4

	Fred's home.
	There is a party in full swing. **Fred** *and* **Elizabeth** *enter in good spirits.*
Fred	Well, well, well! How wonderful it is to have you all here and spending such a lovely day with us. Now how about a little game?
Elizabeth	Is everybody all right for a drink or do you need a top-up? How about you, my love? Would you like a glass of mulled wine?
Fred	No more for Mrs Winterbottom, Elizabeth. I think she's had quite enough already!
Elizabeth	And what about Mr Winterbottom?
Fred	Yes, top him up! He may need it! He can handle his wine!
	The guests laugh.
Elizabeth	There you go, my love.
	Elizabeth *hands* **Mr Winterbottom** *a glass of mulled wine.*
	How about a game? What shall we play?
Party Guest 1	How about blind man's bluff?
Fred	Wonderful, one of my favourites! I'll go first! Come on, Lizzy, where is that blindfold?
Elizabeth	Here we go.
	Elizabeth *gets a blindfold and ties it around* **Fred's** *eyes.*

Can you see anything, Fred? No cheating!

Fred   Who said that?

The guests laugh.

Don't worry, I cannot see a thing, I assure you.

Elizabeth   Well, off you go!

*Music plays while **Fred** staggers around. He finds a party guest. The music stops.*

Fred   Now, who do we have here? Hmmm …

***Scrooge** enters and stands alone. The other party guests see him and their faces fall.*

Well … you could be Mr Bagman? Or you could be Mr Young … you're a tricky one! I think I'll have another go.

***Fred** moves away and discovers **Scrooge**.*

Goodness, you're a bit chilly, aren't you? So, you are a latecomer. This feels like an expensive coat, and a top hat? And what's this? It's a walking stick. Who could you be? Lizzy, give me a clue!

***Elizabeth** stares at **Scrooge**, speechless.*

Come on, just one clue! Lizzy?

***Fred** takes off the blindfold and looks at **Scrooge**. **Fred** cannot believe that **Scrooge** is standing before him. **Scrooge** looks awkward.*

Scrooge   Fred, I … I …

***Scrooge** slowly moves forward and holds out his hand.*

Merry Christmas, Fred.

***Fred** stares at **Scrooge**'s hand, then takes it and shakes it.*

Fred   Merry Christmas, Uncle Ebenezer.

***Fred** and **Scrooge** begin to shake each other's hands. **Scrooge** shakes faster and faster until it seems he will shake off **Fred**'s hand. They laugh heartily.*

The offices of Scrooge & Marley.

Scrooge runs in excitedly, rubbing his hands together. He is wearing his coat and hat. He is also carrying a small wrapped box.

Scrooge Excellent! He isn't here yet. I thought he'd be late and I was right! Too much Christmas cheer and laughing and singing! And turkey no doubt! An army couldn't have finished that bird, but I'll bet young Tim gave it a good go! My goodness, how cold it is in this office! How on earth did I ever get anything done? I should fill the fire with coal and light … no! No, I can't; everything must be as normal. Cratchit must not suspect a thing!

A noise is heard from offstage.

That must be him now!

Cratchit enters slowly and quietly. He advances on his place of work when he is stopped by what sounds like a giggle coming from Scrooge. He looks up and Scrooge immediately buries his head in his work. Cratchit continues to advance quietly and there is another giggle. Again, Cratchit stops and looks toward Scrooge before continuing on his walk. Suddenly Scrooge looks up.

Bob Cratchit! This office has been open for a full fifteen minutes and I do not pay you to turn up late!

Cratchit I'm sorry, Mr Scrooge, it's only once a year.

Scrooge That is a sorry excuse.

Cratchit I'm sorry, sir. I promise that this will never happen again.

Scrooge At least we agree on something, Cratchit. I have just about had it with watching you coming in day in and day out, listening to your teeth chattering and looking over at your miserable face.

Cratchit I'm sorry, Mr Scrooge, I promise … no more teeth chattering. I can do better for you, please!

Scrooge I very much doubt that.

Cratchit	Please, Mr Scrooge, I have a family to support.
Scrooge	I'm afraid it is no good. This situation has to change, I have made up my mind. You are no longer my clerk.

Cratchit drops to his knees, horrified. He looks at Scrooge with his mouth wide open.

However, I am not a man without a conscience. I shall pay you your wage for the day if you can carry out a rather simple and remedial task.

Cratchit	Yes … yes, Mr Scrooge. I … I need the money.
Scrooge	You will screw this new sign to the front door of this establishment. It is to replace the old one that currently sits there. Completion of this task will signal the end of your employment in that position. Do you understand?
Cratchit	Yes, sir.

Scrooge hands Cratchit the small package, which he opens. He takes out of it a brass plaque, which he reads. His mouth drops, again, and he slowly rises. He is in shock.

Scrooge	I take it that the plaque is to your liking, Cratchit?
Cratchit	Mr Scrooge?
Scrooge	The plaque, Bob, is it to your liking?

Cratchit stands and stares at Scrooge.

Why don't you read it? Read it out loud so that I can hear what it sounds like.

Cratchit eventually looks at the plaque again, then back at Scrooge. He looks down and then back at Scrooge, completely stunned.

Well, come along! Nice and loud so I can hear what it sounds like.

Cratchit	*[Reading]* 'Scrooge … Scrooge and … and … and *Cratchit Associates*'? 'Working in the loving memory of Jacob Marley' … I'm afraid I don't quite understand, Mr Scrooge. Does this mean that I can have my job back?

ACT 2   SCENE 5

Scrooge	No, Robert, not at all. You shall have a new job. You are to be my new partner. That is, of course, if you accept?
Cratchit	Well I … I …

Cratchit passes out and Scrooge jumps up in surprise.

Scrooge	Robert! Bob! Good Lord! Are you alright? Cratchit, wake up, wake! I've killed him!

Scrooge kneels down and checks Cratchit's pulse.

Oh thank God, he is still breathing! Brandy! Where is that brandy?

Scrooge runs and grabs a dusty bottle of brandy as Cratchit groans.

Sit up, Bob. Here, drink this.

Cratchit takes one small sip from the bottle and looks at Scrooge. As he focuses on him he pauses before returning to the bottle and taking another large gulp.

Steady, Bob, calm down. I would like for you to be my partner. I think this could be an excellent opportunity for the business, for you, for your wife and for that boy of yours.

Cratchit	My Tim? I'm afraid I don't quite …

Scrooge   Listen, Cratchit . . . I spent Christmas with Fred yesterday. My, what a wonderful Christmas we had, the best I remember in years. Oh, how we laughed! We sang songs, played games, and I'll tell you something, Bob: that Mrs Winterbottom, after a few drinks she got rather overenthusiastic with the mistletoe! But we should keep that to ourselves, I think. More brandy?

*Scrooge picks up the brandy and passes it to **Cratchit**, before continuing.*

I chatted to Elizabeth for hours, what a lovely girl she is! How lucky my nephew is to have a girl like her. She was telling me all about their plans, and their work. They are teachers, you know? Oh! That reminds me, I will need your countersignature for a cheque I'm giving to the school. They need a new roof but I passed that old building this morning and it simply won't do. I have Mr Copley and Mr Jones from the council coming in today to have a chat about putting up a new school. I was thinking about building it up by Green Acres. Do you know Green Acres, Bob? It's a lovely place. I think a school would be perfect up there. What do you think?

Cratchit takes a large swig from the bottle.

Bob Cratchit, you are a fine man, and you have shown devotion and loyalty to me and to this business far beyond what I deserve, and I should like for you to be my partner. What do you say, Bob?

Cratchit   I . . . I think that Green Acres would be a lovely place for a school, Mr Scrooge.

He offers him his hand.

Scrooge   Call me Ebenezer.

*They smile and shake hands. After their handshake **Cratchit** exits.*

*During the following passage **Scrooge** is going around the office getting everything tidied away, locked up, and is blowing out his candles. The **Ghost of Christmas Present** appears behind **Scrooge**.*

Present

Scrooge became as good a man as London had ever known, and to Tiny Tim, who did not die, he became a second father. With Bob Cratchit, he formed a partnership, and a friendship, as good as anyone has ever known. With Fred, he became so close, that people thought them inseparable. No more were those seeking charity scared to approach the doors of Scrooge's office; in fact, it was a first port of call for many, and they never left disappointed. Although many were confused by Scrooge's sudden alteration, many more were just relieved by it. People laughed as rumours of ghosts and goblins reached their ears, but Scrooge let them laugh, as he had grown rather fond of the sound of it. Yes, Ebenezer Scrooge was a changed man, a good man, and everyone was thankful for it. And as Tiny Tim observed, God bless him! God bless everyone!

Scrooge blows the candle out.

Blackout

ACTIVITIES

1   FACT AND FICTION

Like most writers, Charles Dickens (author of the novella, *A Christmas Carol*) used his own life and experiences as material for his stories.

In pairs:

- Read the facts about Charles Dickens and decide how they may have influenced the writing of *A Christmas Carol*. It may help to look at some of the features of the story on page 73.
- Make notes about the links and be prepared to explain them.
- Think carefully about *why* Dickens included these features in his story.
- Present your ideas to the class.

When you are speaking, remember to speak clearly and slowly. It is important to stand still and make eye contact with your audience. When you are listening to others, do not interrupt or distract them.

FACTS ABOUT CHARLES DICKENS

> When Charles Dickens was a boy, his family fell into poverty; he was sent to work in a factory, earning little, and working under dreadful conditions.

> Dickens had mixed feelings about his father. Sometimes he thought he was mean and irresponsible. At other times he thought his father was kind and generous.

> As an adult, Dickens was shocked by the poverty of working people. He campaigned against harsh laws which meant people who lost their jobs were sent to the workhouse or to prison.

Dickens lived in Victorian times, when the festival of Christmas was growing in popularity. Christmas trees were introduced, the first Christmas cards were sent, and the singing of carols became more popular.

Dickens believed that all children should have an education. He believed that ignorance led to poverty and despair.

When he became a successful writer, Dickens raised a lot of money for charities.

Dickens believed that stories could influence people's behaviour and attitudes.

FEATURES OF A CHRISTMAS CAROL

The characters Ignorance and Want are both children.

Happy families celebrate Christmas.

Scrooge has both good and bad in him.

Bob Cratchit is a good man, despite his poverty.

By the end, Scrooge is sharing his wealth and helping others.

A carol singer comes to Scrooge's door.

Charity workers call at Scrooge's work.

ASSESSMENT

- **Self-assessment.** Think carefully about how well you worked with your partner. Give yourself a thumbs up 👍 or thumbs down 👎 as to whether you did the following:
  - shared the reading with your partner
  - listened carefully to your partner's ideas
  - contributed your own ideas to the discussion and notes.

- **Peer assessment.** Ask your 'audience' to give feedback on how you presented your ideas to the class. Ask them to comment on at least two aspects that they felt were good and one that could be improved.

2   WHO AM I?

Check how well you know the characters in this playscript by playing 'Who am I?'

Divide the class into two or three groups. Each group should write down as many characters as they can remember from the playscript.

↓

Check your lists against the list of characters on pages 12–13. Add any characters that you missed out.

↓

Cut the list into individual names. Fold each piece of paper and put them in a box, hat or bag. (Ensure that each group has the same number of character names.)

↓

Sit in a circle and shuffle the names. One person takes a character's name without letting the others see who it is. The others have to guess which character they are by asking questions. The character can only answer 'yes' or 'no'. Here are some example questions:
●   Are you male?
●   Are you a ghost?

↓

Once a character has been identified, that person stands up, but can still ask questions. Before they stand up, they point at another person in the group to take a name from the box.

↓

The first group to have everybody standing up is the winner.

Assessment

- **Self-assessment.** Rate yourself on a scale of 1 to 3 (3 being the highest) for how well you did the following:
  - added to the list of characters
  - listened to what others said about the characters and offered your own ideas
  - asked relevant questions.

- **Teacher assessment.** Ask your teacher to comment on which group worked together most effectively and why.

Freeze Frames

Each group should choose a scene from the play to 'freeze frame'. The other groups have to guess which moment of the play has been 'frozen'.

1   As a group, choose a moment in the play to dramatize. Note that it doesn't have to use all the members of your group, but everyone should help to make the choice.
2   Rehearse the image, discussing the best pose and expression for each character.
3   Talk about what each character is thinking and feeling.
4   Show your freeze frame to the other groups. The other groups can tap one of the actors on the shoulder, then that actor has to say what his or her character is thinking and feeling (without mentioning any names).
5   Can the other group guess which scene you have frozen?

Assessment

- **Peer assessment.** Each group should comment on two things that they felt the other group did well in their freeze frame, and one thing that they think could be improved.

3 EBENEZER SCROOGE

Ebenezer Scrooge is one of the most famous characters in English literature. This is how Charles Dickens first describes him in his novel:

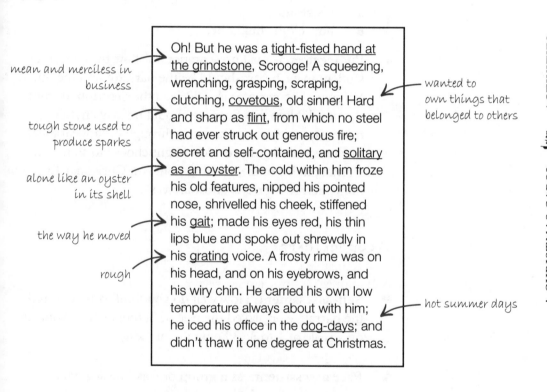

mean and merciless in business

tough stone used to produce sparks

alone like an oyster in its shell

the way he moved

rough

Oh! But he was a <u>tight-fisted hand at the grindstone</u>, Scrooge! A squeezing, wrenching, grasping, scraping, clutching, <u>covetous</u>, old sinner! Hard and sharp as <u>flint</u>, from which no steel had ever struck out generous fire; secret and self-contained, and <u>solitary as an oyster</u>. The cold within him froze his old features, nipped his pointed nose, shrivelled his cheek, stiffened his <u>gait</u>; made his eyes red, his thin lips blue and spoke out shrewdly in his <u>grating</u> voice. A frosty rime was on his head, and on his eyebrows, and his wiry chin. He carried his own low temperature always about with him; he iced his office in the <u>dog-days</u>; and didn't thaw it one degree at Christmas.

wanted to own things that belonged to others

hot summer days

1 Charles Dickens used to tour the country, doing readings of his novels. In pairs, prepare a reading of this passage. Think carefully about:
- which words to emphasize
- where to pause
- how to vary the volume and tone.

Rehearse your reading until you are familiar with all the words, thinking carefully about what they mean.

2   Draw a quick sketch of Scrooge. Use the details given in the text, but you can add some of your own. Label key features.

3   Still in pairs, discuss how you might portray Scrooge onstage. Decide:
- how he might speak
- how he might move
- his facial expressions
- his gestures
- how old he might be.

4   Put together a small presentation to show the class; one student in each pair should be the narrator and the other, Scrooge. The narrator should read the description from the novel. Note that Scrooge should not say anything, but try to convey the character through his appearance, movement and gestures. You might choose to show him working in his office, walking home on Christmas Eve or at home before Marley's ghost arrives.

ASSESSMENT

- **Self-assessment.** How well do you think you delivered the narrative or played the role of Scrooge? Rate yourself on a scale of 1 to 3 (3 being the highest).

- **Peer assessment.** As a group or class, decide which presentation was the best and why.

4 PLAYING WITH TIME AND PLACE

Film directors use 'flashbacks' and 'flashforwards' to take the audience to another time or place in the story. Writers use similar techniques, but often through a character's memories, or a time-travelling device. In *A Christmas Carol*, Marley's ghost arranges for Scrooge to be taken backwards and forwards in time (hoping to teach him a lesson).

1   Check your understanding of the story structure by putting these events in the order they appear in the playscript.

Scrooge makes Bob Cratchit a partner in his business.

The Ghost of Christmas Past takes Scrooge to see a boy in a schoolroom.

Fred and Scrooge shake hands.

The Cratchit family is without Tiny Tim.

The Ghost of Christmas Present takes Scrooge to the Cratchit household.

Mary and Old Joe steal Scrooge's clothes and bedding.

Belle Winklesworth leaves Scrooge.

Jacob Marley visits Scrooge and tells him to change his ways.

Scrooge and Bob Cratchit are working on Christmas Eve.

The children, Ignorance and Want, walk before Scrooge.

Scrooge refuses an invitation from Fred at Christmas.

The Ghost of Christmas Future shows Scrooge a grave.

2   Create a new scene. In pairs, imagine a new final scene in the playscript. It should be set ten years later, again on Christmas Eve. Imagine Scrooge comes back as a ghost to visit his partner, Bob Cratchit. Decide:

- why and when Scrooge died.
- what sort of life Bob Cratchit led after he was made a partner. Did he neglect his family? Was the business successful?
- why Scrooge returns to Bob. Does he have a message? Does he want to show him something or ask him to do something?

When you have decided on these basic ideas, improvise the scene in front of the rest of the class.

ASSESSMENT

- **Self-assessment.** Think about your understanding of how writers can structure their stories. Give yourself a thumbs up 👍 or thumbs down 👎 as to whether you:
  - sorted the events of the playscript into the correct sequence
  - imagined a new scene in the future
  - worked with your partner to improvise a new scene.

- **Peer assessment.** Ask your audience to name two things that they enjoyed about your new scene and one aspect that could be improved.

5 SPOTLIGHT ON LANGUAGE

There are some key words and ideas that run through the playscript (and novella) *A Christmas Carol*.

1 With a partner, read the key words below and match them up to the correct definition.

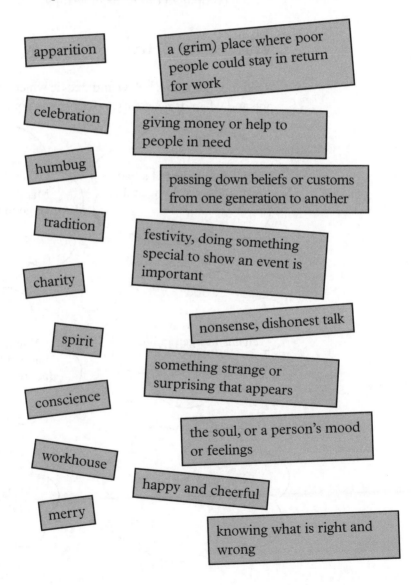

apparition

celebration

humbug

tradition

charity

spirit

conscience

workhouse

merry

a (grim) place where poor people could stay in return for work

giving money or help to people in need

passing down beliefs or customs from one generation to another

festivity, doing something special to show an event is important

nonsense, dishonest talk

something strange or surprising that appears

the soul, or a person's mood or feelings

happy and cheerful

knowing what is right and wrong

2   In pairs, talk about how each word relates to *A Christmas Carol*. It could be a theme; part of the setting; something the characters say, or do, or think about.

3   Each pair should join with another pair. The pairs take turns to choose a word and the other pair have to explain its importance to the story, starting 'I think … is an important word in *A Christmas Carol*, because…'. This can be completed orally, or in writing.

WHO SAYS THIS?

Read the quotations below and decide which character says each one and when. If necessary, refer back to your playscript to check.

I believe he died of a bad heart, and a cruel one at that.

Many would rather die than go to the workhouses.

The chains I wear are the chains I forged in life.

You have become so blinded to anything that does not yield you a profit.

I will drink his health for Father's sake.

Today is the first day of the rest of my life!

Choose a quotation from the playscript that you think sums up the message of *A Christmas Carol* (it does not have to be one of those on page 82). Share it with the class and explain why you chose it.

ASSESSMENT

- **Self-assessment.** Rate yourself on a scale of 1 to 3 (with 3 being the highest) on how well you:
  - understood the key words and ideas
  - explained the importance of the words to the story
  - identified who said the quotations
  - found a quotation to sum up the message of *A Christmas Carol*.

- **Teacher assessment.** Invite your teacher to comment on the class's choice of quotations to sum up the message of the playscript. Discuss which explanations were best and why.

6　Writing a Diary or Blog

1　Imagine you are a character in the play. Write a diary entry explaining:
- the events of the day, including what you did, saw, heard and felt
- what you expect will happen next
- your wishes and fears.

a　First decide which character you are going to be. Think carefully about what that character witnesses and his or her viewpoint.

b　Then decide the moment in the play that you are writing the diary entry for. It could be at the start, part-way through, or at the end.

c　As you write, show awareness of the other characters. You might guess what they are feeling too.

Here are some ideas:

Bob Cratchit on Christmas Eve

Scrooge after Marley's visit on Christmas Eve

The ghost Marley, after visiting Scrooge

Tiny Tim on Christmas Day

Belle Winklesworth, after breaking off the engagement

Bob Cratchit or Scrooge on Boxing Day

Remember
You need to write in the first person, using the pronouns 'I' and 'we'.

2　When you have finished your first draft, swap it with a partner. Ask your partner to point out things he or she feels you have done well, and places where you might be able to make improvements.

Things your partner might look at are:
- spelling and punctuation
- consistent use of the first person (using 'I' and 'we')
- use of paragraphs to divide up the text
- awareness of other characters' feeling and motives.

3 When you have listened to your partner's comments, write a second draft of your diary. Then proofread your text, correcting any errors you find.

EXTENSION ACTIVITY

With a partner, talk about how your diary entry would differ if it were a blog (i.e. a web log on the Internet). Think about:
- the change in audience (who might read it)
- what you might not want to reveal
- what you might prefer to emphasize
- the overall tone of your writing.

You could sketch out a plan for a blog written by Scrooge on Boxing Day, introducing himself and explaining the new outlook for his business: Scrooge and Cratchit Associates.

ASSESSMENT

- **Self-assessment.** Think carefully about how well you worked on your diary entry. Give yourself a thumbs up 👍 or thumbs down 👎 as to how well you:
  - planned your paragraphs
  - wrote in a formal style, using verb tenses correctly
  - checked your spelling and punctuation carefully.

- **Peer assessment.** Give your final draft to a different partner. Ask them to comment on two good things about your diary/blog and one thing that could be improved.

7   CHRISTMAS DEBATE

Some people believe that Christmas nowadays is too commercial. They argue that the focus is all about spending money and getting presents, rather than the traditional celebration for religious or social reasons. Hold a class debate to discuss this. Follow the steps below.

Step 1
Split into two groups: those who feel Christmas is too commercial and those who don't.

Step 2
Appoint a chairperson, who will have the authority to say who can speak and when. You may want your teacher to do this.

Step 3
Each group should appoint a spokesperson to represent their views.

Step 4
Each group should discuss their viewpoint and draw up a list of arguments to support it, using evidence from the playscript where possible (for example the characters' opinions about Christmas). Refer to the 'Things to consider' panel for some ideas, but add more of your own.

Each group should ensure that:
- everyone has an opportunity to express his or her ideas
- everyone listens to what is said and responds to it.

> **Things to consider:**
> - How much money people spend on their children
> - Whether people spend more than they can afford
> - The money made out of making and selling toys, games, decorations – boosting the economy
> - The increase in business for food retailers, hotels, etc.
> - Whether there is too much advertizing
> - Whether it is a good thing for families to get together
> - The value of traditions, such as Christmas trees, etc.
> - The spiritual value of Christmas and other festivals

Step 5
Each spokesperson should give their team's viewpoint. Note that he or she might find it useful to have notes for reference during the presentation.

Step 6
The chairperson 'opens the floor' to other viewpoints – letting everyone have their say.

Step 7
A vote is taken as to whether Christmas is too commercial nowadays. (Note that you do not have to vote with the side that you worked with.) The side with the most votes wins.

ASSESSMENT

- **Self-assessment.** Rate yourself from 1 to 3 (with 3 being the highest) as to how well you:
  - contributed to the group discussion
  - listened to other people's ideas
  - contributed to the debate itself.

- **Teacher assessment.** Ask your teacher to identify three of the strongest arguments put forward in the debate. Ask him or her to suggest ways in which you could improve your debating skills, for example: by doing more background research; by thinking through your arguments more carefully; by listening more closely to what others are saying.

FURTHER ACTIVITIES

1   Imagine you are a publisher and have just been given the manuscript of *A Christmas Carol*. Think of an alternative title, design a cover, and write a blurb to help sell your new publication.

2   What text messages might the ghost of Jacob Marley have sent to his colleagues (the Ghosts of Christmas Past, Christmas Present, and Christmas Future), instructing them how to deal with Scrooge?

3   Imagine Ebenezer Scrooge has asked you to set up a social networking page for him. Sketch one out and decide what details you might change as the play progresses. Include links to other characters and their posts.

4   Think about ideas for an app based on the story; for example, it could be a game based on the characters and themes in *A Christmas Carol*.

5   Hot-seat the character of Bob Cratchit to explore his feelings towards Scrooge. (You will have to decide at what point in the play to interview him.)

6   In pairs, write a rap, a song or a poem to convey the story.

7   In groups, rewrite a scene from a class novel as a playscript. Remember to include character names and stage directions so that actors know how to deliver the lines. When you have finished, swap your scene with another group and feed back on their work, pointing out what you liked about their script and offering advice for improvement. The 'What the Adapters Say' section of the playscript may help with this activity.